All Food Is Good Food

written by
MOLLI JACKSON EHLERT

illustrated by
FANNY LIEM

Feiwel and Friends
New York

When you wake up in the morning
and your tummy rumbles,

that's your body saying,
"Feed me!"

Food gives you the
energy you need to
have fun,

to move and play,

create and explore!

All food has a purpose.
Food does many different things.

Some foods give you energy to wake up.

Others give you strength to do hard things.

Yummy foods make
your taste buds sing.

All food can be delicious.

Foods taste different.
Sweetness may make you dance,

or sourness might make
you pucker with joy.

Spicy foods may tickle your tongue,

and salty ones
might make your
mouth water.

Enjoy the foods
that taste best
to you!

All food powers your day.

Food gives you energy.

Fats power your brain, while carbs power your body.

Proteins make your muscles strong,
and sugar keeps your mood balanced.

Eating many types of food keeps you
feeling your best.

All food brings people together.

Food can connect you to the world.

You can get food
from the ground,

or you can get it
from the store.

Cooking with your family can keep
you in touch with your roots.

Sharing what you make with loved
ones can bring smiles to the table.

All food can have a place in your life.

From breakfast,

to dinner,

and snacks in between,

eat what makes you feel your best.

The foods that make you feel
good are the right foods for you.

All food is good food.

FAQ

for Raising Kids with Food Neutrality

What is Intuitive Eating?

We are born with our instincts around food intact: Our stomachs signal to us when we are hungry and when we are full. As children, we listen to those instincts by nature, but much of our environment teaches us to fight against them. Diet culture runs rampant, sending kids and adults alike the message that we shouldn't listen to our bodies' signals and that we shouldn't eat what we are craving. Intuitive Eating aims to teach adults to get back in touch with these instincts and to encourage kids not to lose them.

Will this make kids think it's okay to eat junk food all the time?

"Junk food" is a phrase that gets thrown around at foods that are mislabeled as unhealthy but often taste *oh so yummy*. Kids think in simple terms, so it's not a stretch to assume that if they like and crave foods that are called "junk" or "bad," they will think they are doing something "bad" by wanting them. Because of this, it's important to treat all food equally when presenting it. We are born Intuitive Eaters, listening to our bodies for what they want and need. Allowing kids to eat without attributing positive or negative qualities to food keeps that intuition intact, letting them learn naturally how different foods make their bodies feel. Eating "junk food" all the time would make you feel sick, and kids will listen to their bodies to avoid that.

Isn't calling all food "good" the opposite of neutrality?

This is a great question, and one I encourage you to ask. In the world of Intuitive Eating nutrition, there is a saying that "all foods fit," but that is a hard concept for young kids to grasp, so saying "all food is good food" puts that concept in terms that they can understand. As a person who grew up with dangerous diet culture in the world, I find it important to challenge the idea that there are such things as "bad" foods. Ultimately, food is good. We need food to function and survive, so that makes it good for us, no matter what kind of food it is.

To future foodies and chefs: Have fun experimenting, creating, and playing with food; I can't wait to see what you come up with! —M. J. E.

To my family, who has always been my unwavering support and encouragement. —F. L.

A Feiwel and Friends Book
An imprint of Macmillan Publishing Group, LLC
120 Broadway, New York, NY 10271 · mackids.com

Our books may be purchased in bulk for promotional, educational, or business use.
Please contact your local bookseller or the Macmillan Corporate and Premium Sales Department at
(800) 221-7945 ext. 5442 or by email at MacmillanSpecialMarkets@macmillan.com.

Library of Congress Cataloging-in-Publication Data is available.

First edition, 2024
Book design by Melisa Vuong
Feiwel and Friends logo designed by Filomena Tuosto
Printed in China by Toppan Leefung Printing Ltd., Dongguan City, Guangdong Province

ISBN 978-1-250-85445-2
3 5 7 9 10 8 6 4 2